Strengthening Hearts and Minds

Strengthening Hearts and Minds

Poems for Children

By
SHARON R. CHACE

Illustrations by
AMY E. CHACE

RESOURCE *Publications* • Eugene, Oregon

STRENGTHENING HEARTS AND MINDS
Poems for Children

Resource Publications
An Imprint of Wipf and Stock Publishers
199 W. 8th Ave., Suite 3
Eugene, OR 97401

www.wipfandstock.com

PAPERBACK ISBN: 978-1-6667-8973-7
HARDCOVER ISBN: 978-1-6667-8974-4
EBOOK ISBN: 978-1-6667-8975-1

VERSION NUMBER 092523

Special thank you to Paul James Miller the creator of the Cadman font which was designed to be highly legible which may prove to be particularly useful to dyslexic readers.

Dedicated to Rosemary Lesch, sister, a dedicated,
seaworthy harbormaster & EMT

Contents

AUTHOR'S NOTE

Some of the poems will be most relevant to children who are more interested in basket design than in basketball. Of course some students enjoy both gym and art. Verse and volleyball are not mutually exclusive. However poetic play offers a counterbalance to sports. My hope is that you will have fun exploring my poems with the children in your life.

Sincerely,
Sharon
Summer, 2023

STAIRS

At
age four
I had to
learn walking down
stairs so family
devised excercises.
Still, at age ten, one step then
stop was slow going down the stairs
in the Pigeon Cove School where no one
would push me down. However I had to
plan well how to best maneuver and therefore
waited to go last or rushed to go first or squeezed
against the railing and wall so others could quickly pass.
Yet I was excellent with crayon, bright, bold, beckoning.

A PORTAL TO CREATIVITY

Picture this, 1954:
Fresh cardboard scent,
a red mini-chest with a
flap that snapped shut
over the top tray filled
with pencils and eraser,
the bottom drawer
with a six inch ruler,
compass and protractor,
suggested compartments
of knowledge in the fifth grade!
Fast forward to 1964:
Math and rulers were not
my tools nor treasures.
But the shape inside
the protractor became
rhythm and design
on a leather tile created
for Art Composition 204.
In time, fifty two years later,
this poem—first draft in pencil.

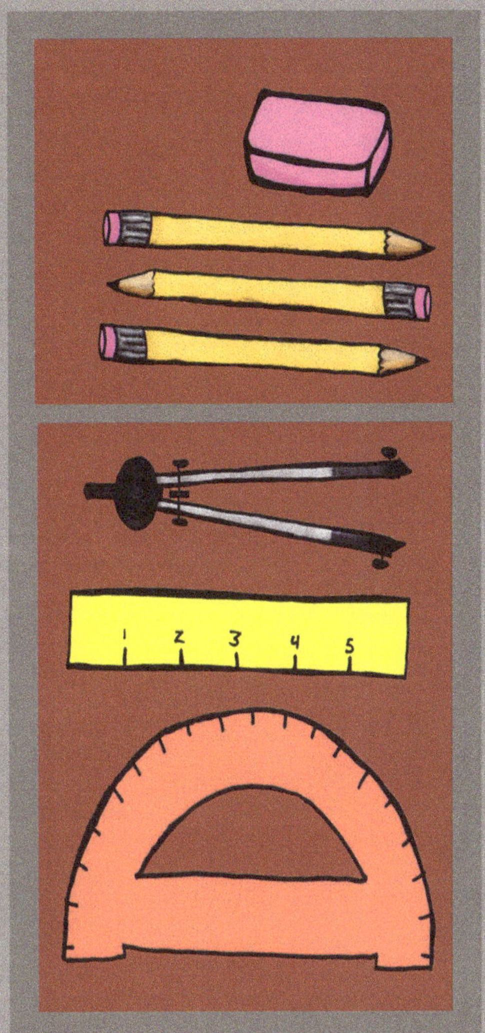

KITTY

If my cat, *Peanut*,
could be a poet,
he would mew
in celebration of
running water,
flowing streams,
and flowering
dogwood in feline
dreams.
Content to be
a writer's cat,
he purrs, intently
looking interested
in computer calamities,
and piles of papers.
Rescued from the shelter,
he now shelters me
with kitty comforts,
interest compounded daily.

TAX TIME

I wish my cat could
help my mother
with the taxes.
He can't because
he is a cat.
After my mom piles
her papers neatly,
he sits on them because
he is a cat.

MORNING NEWS

In the morning
my dad opens
the drapes.
Leaping upon
the table, our cat
looks out the window,
scanning the news
of the day like a person
reading the paper.

IN TIME

When a cat
won't come out
of a closet,
don't coax
her out or forget
and shut the door.
She will come
out eventually—
maybe with kittens.

MIGHTY MORNING

North woods at sunrise;
purple, yellow, orange, pink:
Mountains, mist, moose, Maine.

FRIEND DOG AND BASKETBALL

My team lost the ball game,
but I must say a beagle dog
came to my house to play
and brightened a day
I would have wished away.

TAIL TALES

Lizards have tails.
So do cats and rats.
Surprise, surprise!
Likewise most bats.

BARNYARD DREAM

On a scale from 1 to 10
would you like to ride
a hen?
If you answer 8 or higher
please tell why.
Choose 1 reply.
It would be fun.
I laugh at silly.
I want a hen friend
and will name her
MILLIE.

BIRD OF BROWN FEATHERS

Little brown sparrow,
wild and free,
fly, land, hop, hop, fly
into the safe, spruce tree.
Some birds are bigger
or wear brighter colors
yet you are the dearest
bird to me.

WHAT'S FOR DINNER?

Tired of yogurt,
don't want any
more soup, my father
can't even make
our favorite dish
because the store is out
of all kinds of fish.
So I'll sing to my mother,
"Please, please, please,
there are always baked
potatoes stuffed with
broccoli and cheese."

OTHER SIDE

On the other side of the street
our neighbors have a tree as
perfect as any tree can be.
It stands behind the house
so proud and tall with a
top as round as a basketball,
giving shade to all.
Changing colors through the day—
yellow green, emerald, olive,
lime: It glows at sunset, dress up time,
wearing a green-gold crown.

Parents, sister, brother, dog come
see your maple tree from our yard.
My husband and I will walk
across the street to look at our
window box with marigolds neat.
Looking from different points of
view, is what caring citizens do.

PARKS

Parks are nice.
Parks are sweet.
Parks are full of feet.

Amy Elizabeth Chace
At age 4

CHANGE

After the Rose of Sharon tree
was blown sideways, violets
sprung up in the rich, spring
earth.
With their heart shaped leaves
they seemed to say:
*Change cannot keep all loves
away.*

FOG PARADE

Fog rolls down the street
in a parade of puffs.
Soft mist makes the colors
of the foggy day brighter.
Green grass, speckled salt
and pepper stones, a cardinal's
glistening, red feathers glow.

CHERISHED MOMENT

I tried to find
significance in
attraction,
a dragonfly
landing on my knee.
Maybe insects just
like me.
Affinity is enough.

Learning new words helps young and old poets grow.

Here are the meanings of the big words.

Significance: Important and meaningful

Affinity: Shared attractions, interests, and feelings

APPLE BLOSSOM RHYME

I lifted my little sister
high into the branches
of an apple tree.
Like the girl in a
picture book,
sweet was she,
lovely blossoming
for the world to see.

WARM COLORS

A heat wave came,
turned New England
lawns into Kansas
prairie gold and bronze.

ROSEMARY'S GARDEN

Rosemary's garden flows.
Lilacs, Rose of Sharon, Montauk daisies,
Throughout the seasons and the years,
Gifts of purple, blue, and white,
Lilacs, Rose of Sharon, Montauk Daisies,
Beauty to share and bless,
Gifts of purple, blue, and white,
Loving links to cherished memories,
Beauty to share and bless,
Throughout the seasons and the years,
Loving links to cherished memories,
Rosemary's garden flows.

CHIPMUNK SCAMPERING

When the chipmunk scampers
along the stone wall and the
first orange leaf falls to the lawn,
the breeze is music for the dance.

Montauk daisies in scalloped
edged tutus stretch in arabesque.
The chipmunk pirouettes and leaps off
the wall to dig her burrow in the still
fresh grass. Summer green will not
forever last.

Pellet stove smoke is in the air.
The wind says, "Chipmunks, notice
the swirling milkweed seeds. Gather
quickly for your cache."
Swaying chocolate drop centers of
wilted Black-eyed Susans will soon
have frosty marshmallow toppings.

Standing on the highest stone in the wall, the chipmunk stares as if pondering rhythm. Inside it is time to put the kettle on, gaze at the fire, and join the dance to wonder.

TABLETOP TREE

Tiny tree,
in the window,
our neighbors
will see and smile
with glee.

White lights shine
through the scallop
shells glowing bright
on outstretched branches,
like the Virgin Mary's
arms of loving welcome,
on a white, marble
statue in a churchyard,
a cormorant drying wings
in the ocean breeze,
a child embracing joy
in the world.

TRAIN TALK

Click, click, and clack
the train chatters
on the tracks
all the way to Boston.
I wonder if the stop
called Montserrat
is really named
the MONSTER RAT?

PLAYING

Not too energetic today
that really is okay.
There are many
different ways
to play.
Some children love
to jump and shout
and turn their muscles
inside out.
Others like to pause
and see the wonders
of our world that be.
Thoughts turn into
poetry.

SUN FUN

Squirrels don't need slippers
nor tiny picnic tables built
just for them.
Nevertheless
kindness can bless.
In the pandemic,
grownups made
squirrel friends their
very own little tables.
Playing as children do
is one way to believe
in tomorrow's sun.

SOCKS

Some days are for
warm socks.
Other days you need
them not.
Wrap a box of socks
for someone in need.
Truly indeed
you will sow
a seed that grows
into beauty.

THE START OF ART

It would be nice
to have the biggest
crayon box with
many colors and ten
shades of blue.
But you do not need
all the colors.
All you must have
to be an artist
are the basic tools:
Pencils, sharpener,
eraser, and plain paper.
Add your imagination
to draw, what you see,
what you feel, what you
want.

FRESH AIR FUN

Fly a kite.
Take a hike.
Ride a bike.
See the sights.
Paint what you like.
With all your might
make life bright.

DELIGHT

Greeting Missouri dry heat
with a smile, ten year old
Anna walked into a hayfield
filled with sunshine.
She found field stones and
picked Queen Anne's Lace.
Arranging soft lace among
the hard stones, she took joy.
"For you," she said to the
elderly couple who made
her a home.
"So lovely...How simple,"
they said in reply.
"No need to be fancy."

WOULDN'T IT BE FUNNY?

Wouldn't it be funny if ducks paddled
in puddles with umbrellas under their wings?
Wouldn't it be funny if dogs could fly?
Wouldn't it be funny if turtles could dive?
Now, wait a minute. Turtles do dive.
If they could drive, that would be funny.

Wouldn't it be funny if bunnies took naps
on their very own floral, embroidered mats?
Wouldn't it be funny if horses could count?
Well, some can with their hooves.
Wouldn't it be funny if bears could pout
and turn their frowns upside down when they
found their favorite berries?

Wouldn't it be funny if seagulls could dine
on frosted cupcakes with fish designs?
Wouldn't it be funny if you and I
could put on smocks, imagine that
animals talk and paint their pictures on
old, gray socks?
The writer of this poem is a bit of a goof.
But isn't she funny?

IF GOLDFISH WERE GREEN

My Daddy is Irish
and I do say...
he'd like something
green for St. Patrick's
Day.
I'd give him a goldfish
if goldfish were green.
But have you ever seen
a goldfish of green?
Maybe a green bubble
pipe, not an idea that's
new, or maybe some parsley
in a good Irish stew.
But maybe the pipe and
a stew will not do.
Perhaps I could make
some little green shoes.
I'll think and think not
cry boo hoo.

Soon I will know just
what to do.
I'll look around and find
what is green to put into
a picture on this old
window screen.
Maybe I'll find a
bow of green yarn
or a piece of clover
behind the barn.
A piece of green plaid
left over when my mom
made a suit or a picture of
my brother wearing new,
green boots.
My picture is growing.
Look, here it is done
with most everything green
beneath the sun.

SCHOOL CLUES

Zuri likes spelling best.
She sounds out the words,
gets As on tests. She
could become an editor.
Nadia likes math and more.
She knows that in her future
numbers will last.
She could become a teacher
or an engineer. Cheers!
Albert likes art.
Mixing colors is the
best part. Joy in his heart.
He is already an artist.

Kay likes words
that please her.
Playing with words
is a tease to bring
her feelings out.
She writes poems
and will craft more.
Diane likes basketball.
She sees that playing ball
is not fun for all.
She will be a teacher who
finds a way for all to play.
John likes history.
He considers:
presidents lined up
in a row,
ideas that march on,
even war stories that
make his grandpa sad,
and artists who make people glad.
He could become a professor,
a journalist or an author.

Carol looks at her mother's books about technology. She wants to invent something new. When she grows up that she will do. She will shine as a STEM star. There is a bit of future right here, right now. Your exact work, yourself to be, time will tell. Possibilities will swell. So wish one another well and be pals.

STRENGTHENING

Wishing you all, dear
readers and listeners,
happiness as you
grow and glow,
Sharon and Amy

www.ingramcontent.com/pod-product-compliance
Lightning Source LLC
LaVergne TN
LVHW060632110826
845147LV00014B/901

* 9 7 8 1 6 6 6 7 8 9 7 3 7 *